HOW ~~I QUIT~~ LUCRATIVE MEDICAL CAREER...

And Achieved Financial Freedom Using Real Estate

(You can, too!)

A medical doctor's 22-year journey from orthopedic surgeon to real estate mogul

CHRISTOPHER H. LOO, MD-PhD

Copyright © 2018 Christopher Loo

All Rights Reserved

Independently Published

Paperback ISBN: 978-1-7171-7550-2

Hardback ISBN: 979-8-4264-2570-5

This book is a twenty-two-year work in the making. It is dedicated...

To God. Over the last ten years, You have been there with me, guiding me. Through the trials and tribulations, you have always been there, even though at times it didn't feel like it. Thank you for showing me the path, unfolding Your plan before my eyes, even though I may not know where I was going at times. I know there is much more to come and the future is more abundant than one could ever imagine.

To Mom, Sue Hwa Loo. Although your time on this Earth was short, you showed me how to actually live life. And that life is not measured by your achievements, but by the people who you touch and by creating powerful, positive experiences and memories. I know that you are looking down upon me, protecting me from danger and guiding my steps (even though I may not even realize it).

To my wife, Annie Phu, who has stood by me through all of the ups and downs, trials and tribulations. You have been the voice of reason.

To Dad, Lian-Sim Loo, who taught me the value of hard work, persistence, hustling, and priceless life experiences.

To My brother, Nathaniel H. Loo, MD.

To my nieces, Tiffany, Aubrey, Sofia, Tina, Olivia, and Sabrina, and my nephew, Kai: dream big and bust your ass to make your dreams a reality!

And lastly, to all of the physicians—aspiring, in training, or practicing; those who went into medicine for noble intentions, only to become disillusioned—this knowledge and information is designed for you, to set you free.

Books by Christopher H. Loo

How I Quit My Lucrative Medical Career and Achieved Financial Freedom Using Real Estate (You Can, Too!)

The Physician's Guide to Financial Freedom Using Stocks and Options

The Physician's Guide to Financial Freedom: Getting Started as a Consultant

The Physician's Guide to Financial Freedom: Becoming a Freelance Writer

CONTENTS

INTRODUCTION 3

CHAPTER 1: MY STORY 11

CHAPTER 2: CAREER TRANSITIONS 18

CHAPTER 3: 5 MISTAKES TO AVOID WHEN MAKING A CAREER CHANGE 21

CHAPTER 4: FINANCES 26

CHAPTER 5: ALTERNATE CAREER FIRST STEPS 37

CHAPTER 6: HOW I QUIT MY LUCRATIVE MEDICAL CAREER & BECAME FINANCIALLY FREE INVESTING IN REAL ESTATE 41

CONCLUSION 57

ACKNOWLEDGMENTS 62

ABOUT THE AUTHOR 63

INTRODUCTION

FROM 2000-2007, I thought I had it all. With a 3.98 GPA, awesome MCATs, cutting-edge cancer research, and great interviews, I got into the Baylor College of Medicine in the Houston Texas Medical Center, my first choice. I graduated seven years later with a combined MD-PhD (Bioengineering, Rice University) and matched into an Orthopedic Surgery Residency at New Jersey's Rutgers University.

But, deep down, despite all of these accolades, I was lost, confused, and didn't know what my purpose was in life. I could study the material, learn the facts, sit for exams, see patients, and operate, but I had no passion for the practice of medicine. So, in 2008 (at the peak of the financial crisis), I took a leap of faith, quit my training program, and set out to make it as a real estate entrepreneur and investor.

Fast forward ten years, I am no longer controlled by money. I do not trade my time for money. I work remotely from anywhere in the world, on my laptop, using the Internet. I work for the experience, the education, the learnings, the connections, the stepping stones. I have no boss. I will not deal with or tolerate negativity or drama from others.

I train and run one to two marathons a year. I take multiple vacations a year in different parts of the world. I mentor the younger generation, and I give back to local charities in time, energy, and monetary resources. I am able to enjoy time with my wife and family, read fiction, and watch movies again.

I was not able to do any of this during my medical career, despite the "high" income. But it was not always this way. I have had my fair share of setbacks, frustrations, failures, humiliations, and betrayals along the way. At rock bottom, I can recall sitting alone, hungry, freezing in the East Coast winter, deeply in debt, no assets, with nobody to turn to, and actually contemplating returning to clinical practice! It is because of real estate that I am able to write this book for you.

I have spent the last twenty-two years refining and honing my investment style/strategy. From an early age, I desired and knew I would be financially free. I knew it would be a lot of hard work. I never thought it would be easy. My freedom has come from successfully building multiple streams of passive income using real estate.

I have always been fascinated with real estate. The total control of your destiny and total freedom that comes with success. The many facets and skillsets that one can develop. The total product/service/experience, all in one. The business aspects, the experiences, and interactions with clients.

Through real estate, my passion has been through providing *WOW* experiences. I take pride in taking "ugly" properties and transforming them into gems, providing dazzling experiences that inspire.

Before picture of rental unit living room - 2009

After picture of rental unit living room - 2017

HOW I QUIT MY LUCRATIVE MEDICAL CAREER
(*YOU CAN, TOO*)

Before picture of rental unit kitchen – 2009

After picture of rental unit kitchen - 2017

"Awesome." "Wow. "Beautiful." "Gorgeous." "Eye-opening." These are just some of the adjectives that I hear about my design style and approach to my properties. I love comparing before and after pictures. Each property has a particular theme. I work for an interplay between space and lighting in a modern/contemporary setting.

Having successfully invested in, owned, operated, managed, renovated, and sold over one million dollars' worth in real estate, I will use this book to go through the advantages and disadvantages of real estate investing. I will show you how I went from a shitty surgical resident's salary, staying up 40+ hours straight, working 100+ hours per week and being miserable to increasing my monthly income six times using real estate alone (not including my other streams of income).

I will show you the mindsets required to succeed in this business. I will show you the little tips and tricks needed for success, the pitfalls, and the pathway to success. I will show you how to automate, leverage and scale your business, how to find and attract top-paying, ideal tenants, and how to turn them into long-term clientele. I will show you how to market and advertise your properties using social media, email marketing, and AirBNB for pennies on the dollar! I will show you how to build your "virtual A-team" and how to manage them from anywhere in the world using a laptop, smart phone, and the internet.

My purpose for writing this book is to give back what I know, to expand my reach, get my message out to more people, and help more people.

While real estate is a whole different field than medicine, getting into and completing medical school and then getting into an Orthopedic Surgery Residency taught me a number of skillsets necessary to be successful. These skillsets are useful to any physician contemplating a career change and becoming a real estate entrepreneur.

CHAPTER 1

MY STORY

THIS SECTION IS DESIGNED to give you a background and framework for where I am coming from. I try to offer you, the reader, an objective view so you have some foundational information about how I grew up and where my drives and intentions developed.

Being born on the cusp of both Generation X and Gen-Y had a lot of ramifications on my upbringing and orientation. I grew up in a transitional period when old Industrial Age ideas were colliding with new, Information Age ideas. It was a time when Bill Gates (Microsoft), Steve Jobs (Apple), Jerry Yang (Yahoo), Jeff Bezos (Amazon), MySpace, Facebook,

Napster, Dell, Ebay, Amazon, Google, and Netflix were all coming of age. A time when technology, digitalization, increasing globalization, democratization, demonetization, and dematerialization were leveling the playing field.

It was a time when our social fabric was changing right before our eyes. Industries were wiped out overnight, and new ones came into the fray. Industries such as Blockbuster, Kodak, Toys-R-Us, and K-Mart became obsolete. The United States moved from Super Power to the collapse of the Soviet Union and the rise of China, Russia, Brazil, and India. Our way of life was being disrupted in every way, shape, and form.

This had important implications because, as a second-generation Chinese-American, (like all "ABCs"), we had certain expectations. We were born and had to assimilate into Western culture/Industrial-Information Age society, but we had to adhere to our Asian origins and still establish an identity.

HOW I QUIT MY LUCRATIVE MEDICAL CAREER
(*YOU CAN, TOO)*

It was dichotomous. I never fit in. I was always the outsider, no matter where I went. We enrolled in Saturday Chinese school, studied violin or piano, played tennis, lived in the suburbs with their top-rated free public schools, excelled academically, went to Ivy Leagues, and then went on to become doctors, dentists, lawyers (well-respected professionals), worked for top firms, banks, institutions, and hospitals, lived in affluent neighborhoods, and drove nice cars. Our offspring were expected to continue the same legacy.

This was the definition of "success" placed upon us. We were expected to live by it. Our parents, who came as first-generation immigrants, scrimped, toiled, struggled, saved, and sacrificed for more opportunity for their children. Their identity and self-worth were tied to this narrowly defined concept, attached to their kids' successes and everything it represented.

I grew up around science, medicine, and academia. My parents had masters degrees in microbiology, virology, and veterinary medicine. I competed in science fairs from junior high through high school and went on to do research in the summers in between my undergraduate years. It was all I knew, so I was familiar with it and was able to execute the actions steps necessary to excel in it, but I didn't realize until later in life that I truly did not have a passion for it.

Since my parents were around medical doctors, attendings, department chairs, medical students, residents, and PhDs my natural inclination was to consider medicine as the only career choice. Plus, my mom passed away when I was only eleven years old due to metastatic cancer. That was further fuel for me to go into medicine. I naively thought I could find a cure for cancer and that would solve all of my anger and resentment and make all of the struggle & hardship worthwhile.

As a result, I matriculated at the Baylor College of Medicine in the renowned Houston Texas Medical Center and received a dual MD-PhD degree from the medical scientist training program. I then got into an

HOW I QUIT MY LUCRATIVE MEDICAL CAREER
(*YOU CAN, TOO)*

Orthopedic Surgery Residency at Rutgers University in New Jersey.

While I enjoyed medical and graduate school, my post-graduate medical educational experience was exactly the opposite. While my colleagues truly loved the field of orthopedics, I couldn't stand it. They were willing to undergo the grueling 100+ hour work weeks, stay up for 40+ hours straight, endure the five to six years of training, live on a meager resident's salary, deal with increasing hospital insurance regulations, take on huge medical liability, operate within the inefficient bureaucracy, accept declining reimbursements, and work longer hours *just* to be in the operating room. I, however, could not see myself fulfilling my destiny if I continued on this traditional pathway.

My interests gravitated toward business and entrepreneurship. I found myself reading and studying about real estate, stock investing, options trading, cryptocurrency, creating online digital products and e-commerce in my spare time. Looking back, medical and graduate school taught me the necessary basic skill sets to succeed in life, but I had not truly found my passion.

Questions such as:

- "What does it mean to have 'career satisfaction'?"
- "What is my purpose in life?"
- "What am I meant to do on this Earth?"
- "What do I want to be known for?"
- "How can I leave a legacy?"
- "How can I influence the greatest number of people with the experiences and skill sets that I have?"

As a result of these deep questions and feeling both unfulfilled and lost in my career, I took a leap of faith. I deeply craved for meaning and significance in my career.

The day I turned in my badge and pager and then set out on my own was the most invigorating yet frightening moment of my life. I was leaving a life of stability and certainty, a well-established pathway, for a more uncertain journey. Yet I struck out on a pathway that was potentially more rewarding and offered more growth to me, as an individual.

CHAPTER 2

CAREER TRANSITIONS

HAVE YOU EVER done something truly unconventional, something your parents, friends, and family would call crazy?

Peter H. Diamandis, MD said, "The day before something is a breakthrough, it's a crazy idea!" I couldn't agree more.

Career change is growth, evolution; a process. It will not be perfect or right the first time. Be open to growth, and change during these times. I had the ability to try things differently and approach things in a new way.

HOW I QUIT MY LUCRATIVE MEDICAL CAREER
(*YOU CAN, TOO)*

The traditional medical path can be described as narrow, focused, single-minded, and unidirectional, which is not the way things work in society today.

Nevertheless, veering away from it can be scary and frightening, to say the least. It means you are off the well-beaten path, while your colleagues remain on safe, secure paths and familiar journeys.

If you step off and do something different, you don't fit this traditional mold. Instead, you embark upon your own journey in order to discover your true path, your personal way in the world.

But there are drawbacks! I felt alone, confused, wondering whether I had made the right choice. All of my friends and family called me crazy. Sometimes, your parents disown you! You often feel like nobody is supporting you.

I admit to commonly feeling anger, bitterness, and resentment. I felt like I had spent all of this time, money, energy, and sacrifice only to realize it wasn't worth it. I could see, even when I reached a particular goal, it was never ending. There was a steady stream of licenses, exams, and certifications that had to be addressed in pursuing a traditional clinical medical career.

At the same time, insurance reimbursements were declining and malpractice liability was soaring. Plus there was always politics no matter where you were in the process or profession.

Transitions are never easy. In order to navigate them successfully, I believe you need to have certain things already in place. Career transitions are uniquely hard because we have to let go of our old beliefs, our old selves, and reinvent or recreate ourselves.

CHAPTER 3

5 MISTAKES TO AVOID WHEN MAKING A CAREER CHANGE

AS I SURVEYED MY OPTIONS and began to plan a total career change, I learned some key concepts (some the hard way!). I detail these here, so you, too, can begin to plan wisely, if this route would be best for you.

1. Waiting too long. One of the biggest mistakes I made while making my career transition was waiting too long. Fear held me back. Fear of what people would think about me. Fear of criticism. Fear of failure. Fear that I had invested too much time and energy—all of that studying; all those late nights, interviews, and exams. As a result, I stuck with it, but with each and every day, I felt more and more stuck.

A better approach would have been to take proactive steps. Rather than waiting and waiting, I could have taken a more healthy approach to my career transition. Had I done so, I wouldn't have struggled for so long or wasted so much time and energy. In the long run, I would not have had to endure so much failure, frustration, and humiliation.

2. Not having clarity. This was me. At one point, I wasn't sure if it was the overall career path I had chosen that was off, or if it was just a poor fit. A lot of times, simple adjustments within your current job can make a huge difference. Maybe you don't *have* to leave your current job and start all over. Perhaps all you have to do is make some small changes: having a better attitude; focus on delivering what your boss wants on time; increase the quality of your work output.

At the same time, you need to develop clarity about who **you** are, what you're about, and what goals you want to pursue. This will help you avoid floundering aimlessly about.

I made this mistake. After quitting my residency, I struggled for five years to get back into a different practice, only to learn after three years that it wasn't the fit that was making me unhappy. Rather, the career path in medicine I had chosen wasn't in alignment with what I wanted to accomplish in life. What I *wanted* to be was to be an entrepreneur and investor!

3. Not talking to someone. You don't have to go through it alone. Society teaches us to hold it in, to suppress our concerns and anxiety. Not share it with anyone. We are conditioned to wear multiple masks. You are not supposed to show any vulnerability. You can't show any emotion. If you do, you are weak. You are shamed.

Looking back, one of the best things I could have done would have been to seek out someone sympathetic and empathic to my situation, and to talk through my concerns and fears. However, because of my fear of what other people would think, I waited too long.

As a result, when I finally made my career transition, it was a lot rockier than it would have been, had I confided in someone ten years before and talked about my worries and challenges. I thought it was taboo to talk about these things and hard to find people who had been through the same things as I. These days, though, there are plenty of people who are going through the same experience as you are. So please, seek them out!

People I highly recommend, as a way to get started, are either Pam Pappas, MD or Heather Fork, MD. They were both instrumental in helping me make the major transition in my career.

4. Thinking that you are alone. See points #1 and #3.

I will say this from personal experience: *you are not alone.* There are a lot of people who are going through the same issues and dealing with the same process as you are. I learned that, "the more personal the struggle, the more universal it is".

5. Thinking during your career transition, that you are a "failure,". I felt this for a long time. As a result, I was angry, jaded, and insecure. I often felt I was just not good enough. A more healthy approach would be to view your transition as a period of personal growth onto bigger and better things (which turns out to be the case). Again, we live in a society that paints a picture of life as smooth, steady, and easy, with no bumps in the road.

CHAPTER 4

FINANCES

WHEN I WAS FIVE years old, my dad would take me to the homeless shelters, where we would volunteer during Thanksgiving and Christmas, feeding the poor and hungry. He would always say, "You think you have it bad, but ninety percent of other people have it even worse."

He did this to teach me lessons about gratitude and appreciation for what I had; to make use of every day and every available moment; and to utilize what talents and resources I had to provide value. He took me to the shelters and breadlines to experience what it was like, implying, if I didn't work hard, I would be in the same position as many of those individuals. He taught me not to think of myself as a victim or entitled. He wanted to empower me to be, do, and have more.

The sad reality in the United States is that the majority of society's members are broke, poor, and unhealthy. Many are living paycheck to paycheck. During my medical career, I saw this first-hand: morbid obesity, diabetes, poverty, and serious lack of resources. Many on government programs that did little or nothing for them. Denial, giving up, running away were common symptoms because they knew they were in dire straits. Many patients refused care. It was disheartening to see the gap between rich and poor widen every year.

I vowed to myself I would never be in such a position, and that I would strive to give back to society in the form of service and education. But I wondered constantly: why is it that the richest country in the world can have so many people who are helpless, hopeless, and destitute?

The sad truth is that our education system, health care system, and government programs are *far* behind where they need to be. They were created for Industrial Age ideas and practices. They haven't been revamped or updated for the twenty-first century. We live in a "get rich quick" society. We live in a consumerist society. We have a "keep up with the Jones" mentality. We think winning the lotto will solve all our problems—despite the fact that the majority end up worse than where they started. We believe in "overnight success," rather than understand it takes years, even decades of failure and struggles to accomplish something significant and great.

We now live in the Information Age, which has been dubbed the Creative Age, the Sharing Economy, the Gig-Freelance Economy, Internet 3.0, Age of Millennials. How the Industrial Age commoditized physical labor, the Information Age is commoditizing knowledge, information, and mental labor. Ideas about work-life balance, education, family, and relationships have drastically changed. Therefore, creativity, innovation, and other specific, unique non-traditional skill sets are of utmost importance in the upcoming decades.

HOW I QUIT MY LUCRATIVE MEDICAL CAREER
(*YOU CAN, TOO*)

In the Industrial Age, it took DECADES to become a millionaire, and most of them were in their sixties and seventies, after climbing the corporate ladder. These days, we have twenty- and thirty-somethings who have amassed millions in YEARS, sometimes in even less time, and many without a traditional "job." There are now teenage millionaires and twenty-something billionaires. They've learned how to leverage information, the Internet, and technology, and know how to market and brand themselves and their ideas.

That's how fast things have changed. If you are to survive in today's society, you need to change and adapt *fast* and get rid of old, ineffective, and outdated ideas.

Our programs and institutions remain extremely bureaucratic, slow, inefficient, and ineffective. Corporate marketing and advertising campaigns, along with politicians, want to keep us in the dark and preserve the status quo, so they can remain in power and control.

In today's economy, it has never been more important to teach individuals the importance of financial literacy.

In terms of finances, you need the following three buckets for asset allocation:

1. Savings-emergency: Each and every month, 33% of your paycheck should go to this "bucket." This is a percentage of your total monthly income (either passive or from a business or job). I believe you should maintain savings in the amount equal to at least two years' income, just in case, but most financial advisors recommend three to six months' worth.

2. Growth-investment: 33% of your paycheck should go to a growth/investment vehicle. Rather than consume, become an owner/investor. Do you like your Apple iPhone? Buy some Apple stock. Do you think your bank charges fees that are too high? Invest in the stocks of publicly traded companies (e.g., Starbucks, JP Morgan, ComCast, Verizon). These are true stories of how I chose some of my investment vehicles. The essence of this philosophy is: don't be a consumer. Be an owner/investor!

When you are allocating this bucket to investing, note we are not *trading. We* are *investing.* In Tony Robbins's book *Unshakeable,* he interviews billionaires, people who have made their money investing and trading. Here are a few of the key points they make:

A. The stock market will always go up over time, unless economic activity ceases. These uptrends will always be accompanied by corrections (10%) and bear markets (20%). The key here is the amount of time it takes to get out of these cycles. So, the best strategy for your growth/investment vehicle is regular, periodic purchases of index funds (with low fees), which will average out as positive income over the long run (dollar cost averaging).

B. There is, on average, a market correction every year and it lasts for several months.

C. A bear market occurs every three to five years and can last anywhere from several months to several years. These are the times when, if you have done your homework and research, and are prepared, you can capture market share unlike any other time in the history. Think about the recessions/bear markets of 2001 and 2008, or the great bull market since 2009 up to now.

D. Additionally, reinvest your dividends back into the fund, for compounding, exponential returns.

3. Dream bucket: Everyone has to have dreams. Money is a tool or a resource to be used for good here on Earth. It should not to be amassed or hoarded, only to be left here when we finish our lives. So, what is your dream?

Dream Big, like Peter Diamandis, Grant Cardone, Elon Musk, Richard Branson, Jeff Bezos, or Larry Page. Take your idea and think ten-times bigger, whatever your dream is. So, if you want to be a millionaire, think about having $10 million in the bank.

Avoid average, normal plans and ideas for this aspect of your financial planning. We live only once, so why not take risk, grow, learn, and develop? The biggest risk is not taking one at all, fearing failure, and living with regrets (lost opportunity is greater than trying and failing.) There will be "failures" along the way, but they are only failures if you quit, if you stop learning and growing. These setbacks are stepping-stones. They provide feedback for how to get you to where you need to be.

Dreams and desires are what the universe has already told you what is possible; what you *can* be, do, accomplish, and have. You just have to apply consistency and dedication toward your goals. Work hard on your goals every single day, as Denzel Washington says.

Here are some of mine:

1. Own a private jet.

2. Own a private island

3. Have courtside seats to all of the best events.

4. Be generous with others.

5. Start a charitable foundation: help one million at-risk youth reach their dreams and fulfill their potential. Support anti-bullying efforts. Take on the

NRA. Take on Big Pharma. Reform the health care system. Reform the education system. Feed a million hungry people. Help a hundred families out of poverty, through mentoring and education.

6. Take a trip to outer space.

7. Meet Richard Branson, Elon Musk, Warren Buffet, Jeff Bezos, Larry Page. Have lunch with some of the top influential minds, like Tony Robbins, Oprah, and Peter Diamandis.

8. Start a school teaching financial education, life success, and entrepreneurship.

9. Become a billionaire.

###

Dreams get you out of bed every day. Dreams get you up and going, moving forward with purpose. They inspire your passion.

So, what is your dream bucket?

HOW I QUIT MY LUCRATIVE MEDICAL CAREER
(*YOU CAN, TOO)*

2018 Trip Through Thailand

2018 Trip Through China

CHAPTER 5

ALTERNATE CAREER FIRST STEPS

NOW THAT YOU, the reader, have a sense of where I am coming from, know some of the most common issues when making a career transition, and are ready or in the process of positioning yourself financially, I will go into the nuts and bolts of actually stepping out, making the leap, and venturing into the realm of real estate.

Let's say you are interested in alternative careers. Or maybe you are interested in developing a side gig, an alternative stream of income. Some physicians quit cold turkey, while others make the transition gradually.

Either way, the basic premise for career transition is how sound and well-off you are financially, so you can make this change. That is why examining your personal finances is so important.

Let's look at the typical components:

- House payment—this should be no more than a third of your paycheck.
- Car payment and insurance
- Student loan repayment
- Kids—including activities, tuition for private schools, and financing undergraduate education
- Spouse

The fewer obligations you have and the more income/assets/savings you have, the better off you will be, going into a career change.

You are getting ready to take the plunge. It can be quick or gradual, but it will invariably be all the better for proper planning ahead. Here are several rules I have lived by that have kept me better off:

- **Debt**: Society teaches us we need a mortgage on a house, and we need to go further into debt by buying a car, taking out student loans, buying on credit. However, the world is changing and this is already old, outdated advice. Some of these ideas and concepts may still ring true, but taking on debt to your advantage applies only to certain situations, circumstances, but not *all* of them anymore. (So much for the fifties-era "American Dream" construct). In my opinion, and certainly as you strategize a career change, the less debt you have, the better.

- **Income:** If you do have debt, the more income, savings, and assets you have that can service that debt, the better. In summary: carry little to no debt **or** have consistent passive income that can service the debt.

- **Passive Income:** The more passive income you have coming in each month, the closer you will be to becoming financially free. Passive income is particularly powerful because it removes you and the need for your time from the equation.

- **Savings**: It is recommended that you have three to six months' worth in savings. Personally, I recommend two to three years' worth, due to the uncertainty out there in the market.
- **Paying down debt/building up passive income:** If you have a high ratio of debt to income (i.e., >2:1), a better step to career change is a gradual transition, pay off some of that debt. Start working on residual income streams, too. My personal recommendation is to spend one hour each day focusing on building passive, residual streams of income (e.g., real estate, dividend-producing stocks, options, books, vlogging/blogging, social media, consulting business). This strategy will steadily get you closer to transitioning or to incorporating it into your medical career.

CHAPTER 6

HOW I QUIT MY LUCRATIVE MEDICAL CAREER & BECAME FINANCIALLY FREE INVESTING IN REAL ESTATE

SO, HOW DO YOU KNOW if you're a good fit for real estate?

Real estate may be a good fit for you if you have:

- Personality style
  - Complete control
  - Value of your time
  - Flexibility
  - People-driven
  - "WOW" factor
  - Building businesses

- Managing/leading teams
- Installing systems
- Managing risk
- Skillset and experience
    - Negotiation
    - Finance
    - Design and decoration
    - Renovating
    - Creation
    - Staging
    - Realtor
    - Innovate
    - Create
    - Marketing and advertising

Below are the advantages and disadvantages of investing in real estate:

Advantages:

- 100% control
- Vehicle
    - All-inclusive
    - Passive income

- Tax advantaged
- Hard asset
  - Appreciation
  - Depreciation
  - Cash flow
- Flexibility
  - Part-time
  - Full-time
  - Multi-faceted, roles
  - Amount of involvement
  - Employees

Disadvantages:

- 100% responsible
  - Natural disasters
  - Disasters
  - Liability
  - Tenants
    - Non-payment
    - Damage
    - Theft
    - Eviction

Now I will take you through my step-by-step, cookie cutter approach to real estate investing.

1. Decide where you want to be.

Decide what zip code you want to invest in, what geographic areas you want to invest in. Real estate is all about location, location, location.

Things you want to look for in areas are:

a. Good schools
b. Neighborhoods with access to amenities, like grocery stores, gyms, gas stations, restaurants.
c. Median income of the inhabitants of the areas.
d. Race, gender, sex, marital status, occupations of the population
e. Population growth should be increasing (good research data available on www.BestPlaces.net)
f. Crime rate and the types of crimes
g. Weather year-round

A word of caution when you are investing in transitional cities or cities traditionally known for high crime rates, poor education, and/or a high drug rate. While you may think you can find good deals here, from an investment perspective, the truth is that these places are cheap/low-priced for a reason.

Many times, you will be able to acquire and even renovate or improve a property there, only to find you may have difficulty renting it out or selling it because of the negative connotations of the location.

Unless you can weather the down times, I recommend staying away from these properties, which are purely speculative (e.g., in Detroit, Baltimore, Oakland, Newark). In these instances, you are betting on the city turning around or becoming the "next big thing," like a Hoboken, Austin, or Charleston. While investing in these speculative cities may be potentially lucrative, they may be highly risky, as well. Buyer beware.

Personally, I invested Newark, New Jersey. I bought a decent one-bedroom condominium outside of New York City, in a city known as being impoverished over the last few decades. The building and unit themselves were decent: the place needed some improvements, but nothing that couldn't be done. The area was "up and coming": it was centrally-located, had easy access to schools, hospitals, major transit hubs, and close to Manhattan. I was betting on the rents in New York City eventually being too much for people, so they would need places to stay outside of the city. And that Newark would become a popular hub.

And now—it is! It served as my home base during my residency training. It gave me the chance to learn tenant management skills, renovation, to learn how to manage a business without me being physically present (i.e., a business owner versus a business operator/manager), and at the same time how to speculate on these factors.

That said, I do not recommend taking this approach, if you are a beginning investor. Looking back, though, my Newark investment has given me a lot of experience and education. I would do the same thing over, but at a different point in my life.

2. Once you figure out your desired zip code, next determine how well you are positioned as an investor.

a. Where are you located? I recommend living in the city (within a five- to ten-mile radius) where you want to or decide to invest. Avoid out-of-state city investments, unless you can get an excellent property management company or can manage the property remotely, because rental investment properties take a lot of time and energy (e.g., flying, time, resources).
b. How much capital do you have access to? Are you going to go all-cash financing? Or are you going to go with bank financing?
c. Are you a full-time investor? Or investing part-time?
d. How much involvement do you want in your property, day-to-day? Do you want to hand it over to a management company?) And what parts of the business do you want to be involved with? (e.g., tenant screening, interviewing, marketing, social media, renovations/upgrades/repairs, financing, property management).

Personally, I like to be involved in the tenant screening and interview process, as I enjoy the experience of meeting potential clients, getting to know them, providing them with an unbelievable experience, and developing close relationships with my clients. I also like the marketing and social media aspects, like creating videos and photos that are posted on my website and on AirBNB. I also enjoy the final product, seeing the final home after a huge renovation project.

e. How much manpower, talent, time, and resources do you have? I recommend that you build a team that includes the following:
- A realtor with an investing mindset or background
- A preferred title company and closing location
- A general contractor
- A property managing company,
- A payment solution—there are many free, cheap ones; I personally use

AirBNB to advertise all of my properties. It is a great platform, easily scalable, and it reaches the masses easily. I can use my own photos and videos to market "experiences" to potential clients. It has built-in messaging/inbox and trust-verification features. It handles all of the payments, too, so you don't have to hear the old adage, "The check is in the mail."

- A lawyer with tax accounting and liability experience
- A tax accountant
- An inspector
- An appraiser, if you are using bank financing
- An insurance agent
- A trusted advisor or confidant, to bounce ideas off of
- Someone who is "handy" in repairs – electrician, plumber, A/C, washer, dryer.

Renovations, upgrades, and repairs can be a hassle at times, but they are a necessary component of the timeline of a property. They take up a lot of time, energy, capital, and manpower, but I love taking a literal "piece of shit" property and doing the necessary work to make the place look, "*WOW*!" It is hard work but worth it, and it pays off in the end.

3. Look at "days on market (DOM)". Places with <30 DOM are in a "flipping" cycle, and DOM >30 are for rentals.

4. Prices: should be no more than three-times the median income of the area or location you are targeting.

5. Target properties that cater to single families (i.e., three bedrooms, two baths). This is the type of investment that the median population is looking to buy in.

6. Once you have the zip code and price, go to www.realtor.com and start the "funneling" process. For every one hundred properties you see, make twenty offers. Of those twenty offers, four will be accepted, and one will go to closing. This is the most important part of the real estate investing process, because it develops and hones your skill as an investor.

During this step, you are looking for value: what can you get for how much and how much it will take to give X to your tenant (i.e., buy low and improve).

It will also let you know how much you need to spend to get X amount of value, and what areas of the home improvement process deliver the most bang for the buck (e.g., kitchen, bathroom).

You must take MASSIVE, *MASSIVE* amounts of action. The more action you take—doing research, going out and seeing properties, determining what the value is, determining how much value you can put into the property, and making offers—the better investor you become.

7. You got the offer, contract signed. You did the inspection. You went to closing. **CONGRATULATIONS!**

Now that you have control and ownership of the property, the fun begins. Start asking these questions and exploring these options:

- What improvements or renovations do you want to make to the property?
- How much capital do you have and how do you want to allocate the funds? Towards new flooring? New kitchen? The highest bang-for-your buck improvements occur in the kitchen and bathroom, so place your focus there.
- Do you want to furnish the place? How do you want to furnish it (i.e., what style, quality)?
- What target niche do you want target? For example, I target up-and-coming professional clientele, visiting doctors, medical students, postdocs, grad students, and scientists. Also, unless you are dealing with single/solo males, a lot of the purchasing decisions (the decision to buy, the decision to rent from you) will most likely be by women, so cater to them as

buyers. Target your marketing toward the female population. Highlight aspects of your space that are spacious, bright, clear, clean, and fresh.
- How do you want to reach these target niches? Using word of mouth? Email lists? AirBNB?

This is perhaps the most exciting part of the journey, as there are infinite possibilities.

8. Automation: Once you have acquired the property, it is now a potential asset that you can use to generate passive income. When I say passive income, there is still "work" to be done. The similarity is that you must put a significant amount of time, effort, focus in providing value, delivering the product/service. The only difference is that unlike a traditional job, you can do that in a variety of ways. Either sweat equity or outsource the various projects/jobs/roles within the unit (i.e., "business").

Starting out, you are the owner, operator, and manager. However, you can outsource a lot of the operations (property manager, contractors), so that you are left with the essentials (i.e., you are becoming a business owner—working on your business, establishing systems, processes (owner), vs. working in your business (manager, operator)). And you are left with tasks and responsibilities best suited to your personality style, skillset, interests, strengths. In my business, I have zero employees, I am not very handy, but I hire contractors whenever I need something done (e.g., A/C, heating, plumbing, repairs, renovations, upgrades).

One of the coolest developments in our day and age is the use of technology to automate a lot of the repetitive tasks/processes that would normally be carried out by people. For example, a platform I use (no people) to automate many of my rental units is AirBNB. AirBNB functions as a platform for scaling reach, trust, handles payments securely, accurately, and allows you to message communicate with guests.

- Tired of late payments from tenants?
- Tired of high PayPal, credit card fees?

- Not sure who to trust?
- Interested in photography, marketing, the experiential culture?
- Interested in meeting, getting to know guests from all over the world.

AirBNB has addressed all of these concerns, upfront, for a small nominal fee. Some of the cool automation business tools include:

- The ability to create automated message templates—so that you don't have to re-type the same message over and over.
- You can create cool greeting messages, videos, check-in, check-out instructions.
- AirBNB also has a 1 million dollar insurance policy should you encounter any issues where "guests" destroy/damage your property knowingly or unintentionally.
- Co-Host—you can work with other hosts in the area to meet/greet/say farewell, collect keys, perform the cleaning. You can also apply to be a co-host yourself.

- Special listing status - w/Instant Book, or AirBNB Plus.

I have used AirBNB successfully to manage my out-of-state properties in New Jersey and Las Vegas —all using AirBNB automation. That is the power of technology!

As Keith Cunningham (*Keys to the Vault* and *The Ultimate Blueprint for an Insanely Successful Business*) and Tony Robbins said: "Become a business owner—one who establishes systems, processes to remove himself from the equation, so that the business can run on its own without you being there. Don't become a business manager, operator. That requires your time and effort and for you to be there 24/7. Great operators/managers get tired, great business owners get rich."

CONCLUSION

THIS BOOK IS the culmination of twenty-two years' worth of experience in investing, career transitions, business, and finance. It comes after six years of dabbling, experimenting on the side, and the transition from a "traditional" medical career to a full-time, six-figure passive income using real estate.

When I first started my journey toward becoming a full-time entrepreneur, investor, and businessman, I only had books and ideas from many success-minded individuals. I had nothing but ideas and a desire and a drive to do and be something successful. A creation in my own right. Fast-forward to ten years later (2018), the world is changing right before our eyes. We now have tribes and communities. It has become easy to find those who are looking for the same things as you.

I wrote this book for two reasons. First, to reach those of you who have been "blinded" by society—by its marketing and advertising; brainwashed into thinking society needs us to be or should be a certain way. Our traditional health care system is so narrow-minded and risk-averse, perhaps you believe you can only work in a hospital-based setting to be successful. And since they don't teach the business side of things in medical school, doctors often know nothing about how to start, run, manage, and own a business, so they too often become slaves to true businessmen.

The second reason I wrote this was to solve my own question: why did I enjoy medical and graduate school but hate every minute of residency and clinical work?

Through the years, I have learned that once you have achieved a level of success, you have to give back. This is through charity, philanthropic works, or community service. It is also a responsibility to

HOW I QUIT MY LUCRATIVE MEDICAL CAREER
(*YOU CAN, TOO)*

inspire people under you, by educating and mentoring them, making them successful. This can be done through books, audiocasts, videos, seminars, courses, or programs.

This success did not come without a *heavy* price tag. Struggling with fear (fear of failure, success, criticism, missing out, not being enough, regretting the past, fearing the future). Battling loneliness, no one to turn to, no one to relate to, self-doubt, and insecurity. It was ten years of struggle, feeling lost, empty, like I was failing.

Many times, I questioned whether I had made the right choice. My friends, family, colleagues thought I was crazy. Some of them walked away, never to be heard from again (so they're not my true friends).

It was exhilarating yet frightening at the same time. It was a struggle, but I came out stronger, better for it. I am able to weather uncertainty, failure, risk, and humiliation much better and with ease. What started out as a struggle became a path to truly becoming free and fulfilling my true potential/destiny.

You see: I never would have reached the level of success I have now had I not faced my fears head-on, despite how challenging that was. If I had held onto and lived out the expectations placed upon me, I wouldn't be here. If I hadn't realized that caring about what other people who I barely knew thought of me, I couldn't be here. I learned that needing others' approval and validation was detrimental to my destiny. And that I would rather die trying and failing than sit back, watch, and wait in fear as my life passed me by, while others were out chasing their own dreams and ambitions.

This book was inspired by my desire to give what I have gotten. I am grateful for the opportunity you have given me to serve you in your pursuit of success. My success has been the result of hardship, failures, embarrassments, frustrations, setbacks, humiliation, betrayal, and defeats, as well as the desire to never stop growing, contributing, and giving. I am grateful you chose to invest your time with me and this book. I hope that this book was able to inform and inspire you.

- To your continued success!

ACKNOWLEDGMENTS

A SPECIAL THANK YOU to:

All of my mentors (in person and in spirit), whose words and actions inspired me to dream and think the impossible (in no particular order): Brian Tracy, Robert Kiyosaki, John Maxwell, Tony Robbins, Oprah Winfrey, Jeff Bezos, Elon Musk, Richard Branson, Napoleon Hill, Bill Gates, Deepak Chopra, Zig Ziglar, Steve Jobs, Grant Cardone, Wayne Dyer, Jack Canfield, Timothy Ferriss, Tai Lopez, Christopher Kai, and others!

ABOUT THE AUTHOR

DR. CHRISTOPHER LOO is a physician who became financially free at the age of twenty-nine and retired early at the age of thirty-eight, as a result of making strategic investments after the 2008 financial crisis. A graduate of the MD-PhD program offered jointly through the Baylor College of Medicine and Department of Bioengineering at Rice University, he is the author of *How I Quit My Lucrative Career and Achieved Financial Freedom*

Using Real Estate and three other Physician's Guides for financial freedom. He is the host of the *Financial Freedom for Physicians* podcast, a regular contributor to KevinMD, and has spoken about the importance of financial literacy for Passive Income MD, the White Coat Investor, Board Vitals, SEAK Non-Clinical Careers, SoMe Docs, Doximity, Medpage Today, FinCon, and other high-profile financial brands geared toward high-income professionals.

His website is www.drchrisloomdphd.com.

Chris can be reached at chL1357@gmail.com or you can follow him @

LinkedIn: Christopher-h-loo-md-phd

FB: @drchrisloomdphd @chL1357

Tw: @chL1357

IG: @chL1357

YT: @chL1357**napChat:** @chL1357

Made in United States
North Haven, CT
16 January 2023